undivided

LIVING for AND NOT JUST with ONE ANOTHER

Mitchell & Rhonda Owens

Undivided: Living For and Not Just With One Another
Mitchell and Rhonda Owens
©2015 Mitchell and Rhonda Owens

Table of Contents

Acknowledgements

YEARS AGO, MY FRIEND MICHELE HOWE patiently sat down with me (Rhonda) to explain the business of freelance writing. Just stepping out of my position as a high school English teacher and into the position of new mom, I relished the idea of putting my brain to work between diaper changes and board books, park visits and play dates. Shelly's kindness in spending several afternoons with me—a stranger!—encouraging me and cheering me on, gave me the courage to begin writing. Without her, I'm not sure I'd have the nerve to call myself 'writer.'

Now—15 years, a move to the Pacific Northwest and back, the launch of a non-profit organization, a career change and two children later—Mitchell and I also owe a great deal of gratitude to friends Patrick and Ruth Schwenk.

Patrick—pastor, writer, and teacher—is masterful at breaking down intellectually heady material into manageable and memorable bits and pieces. He's also a creative-type, always coming up with enticing sermon series, beguiling book titles, and thought-provoking blog posts. It is because of Patrick that we began writing this devotional, on this topic, with these Bible verses. Thank you for the inspiration, Pat!

undivided

Ruth—creator of *TheBetterMom.com* and, with Patrick, *ForTheFamily.org*—graciously instructed us regarding behind-the-scenes administration surrounding eBook creation, social media marketing, blog posting, contribution Web sites, platform building, etc. Anyone in the publishing industry understands that times have changed tremendously over the last 15 years, and Ruth happily shared (and continues to share) her expertise with us.

Also, Jeff and Joy at Five J's Design have been so very professional and patient with us! We have thoroughly enjoyed working with them as communication has been quick and concise, and their work has been thorough and distinctive. We highly recommend Five J's Design for eBook and graphic design needs.

Finally, we wouldn't be writing this at all if it weren't for our loves: Autumn and Eden. The two of you made our family complete, and our family has—indeed!—been a training ground where we continue to learn how to live for one another and not just with one another. Our prayer is that we may forever live as a family undivided.

Welcome

WE LIVE IN A CULTURE where people are pulled in a thousand different directions. With so many distractions, it's easy to live in the same house with children and a spouse without really engaging them in deep relationship.

In other words, if we're not careful, family members could become mere roommates—people whose paths we cross for a few minutes at breakfast, and maybe a few more minutes before bedtime, but no one with whom we develop any real connection.

To counter this negative trend we humbly present *Undivided*, a devotional written to help you live *for*, and not just *with*, one another as a family.

Because the good news is this: God has purposely given our families to us as a gift. We aren't meant to just "get along" with each other. No. God's heart is that we would be families that live *for* each other.

Jesus said, "A new command I give you: Love one another. As I have loved you, so you must love one another. By this everyone will know that you are my disciples, if you love one another" (John 13:34-35).

undivided

And where is the training ground for showcasing the kind of love about which Jesus teaches?

The family.

Your family, and ours.

Because a family that lives for one another and not just with one another is a family that remains... *Undivided.*

Overview

IN THE NEW TESTAMENT, there are a variety of "one another" passages—verses that describe various ways we should live Jesus' command to "love one another."

Undivided is a 12-week devotional that the whole family will study together. To that end, each chapter of *Undivided* contains four sections:

LEARN IT: Examine the context of the "one another" passage to understand the original author's intent.

LIVE IT: Determine how to apply the "one another" passage in your home through a practical devotional reading.

ASK IT: Gain deeper understanding of the material through discussion questions that will help all members of the family—from the very young through teenagers—explore biblical truths.

GIVE IT: Personalize the passage by completing hands-on activities and object lessons to develop specific ways in which to live for members in your family and to give away the biblical truth to others.

undivided

A possible study schedule for *Undivided* could be as follows:

MONDAY – Read the "Learn It" and "Live It" sections. Begin working on memorizing the key verse (or verses) for that particular week.

WEDNESDAY – Discuss as a family the questions in the "Ask It" section, and continue memorization.

FRIDAY – Reread the key verse (or verses), and complete the activities in the "Give It" section.

This timeline is just a suggestion. There is no right or wrong way to study through *Undivided*. Each family is different, so feel free to have fun and make it your own.

Ultimately, our prayer is that your family will grow into people who intentionally live *for*—and not just *with*—one another.

Enjoy!

Lesson One:
Love One Another

KEY VERSE

My command is this: Love each other as I have loved you.

~John 15:12

LEARN IT

SPOKEN BY JESUS HIMSELF, this key verse is part of what is sometimes referred to as the "Farewell Discourses" because when Jesus shares these words, He knows that the day He will die for the sins of the world is quickly approaching. In essence, Jesus is trying to prepare His disciples for His departure.

John 13:1 says, *"It was just before the Passover Festival. Jesus knew that the hour had come for him to leave this world and go to the Father."* Because "the hour had come" for Jesus "to leave this world," He not only wanted to make sure the disciples understood *why* He was leaving; He also wanted to teach them *how* to live in His absence.

So how were the disciples—and essentially all believers—to live after Christ's death and resurrection? Simply put, they were to live in love; they were to do *all* things in *love*.

And that is exactly how we are to live as well, especially in our families. But this love is much stronger than just a feeling or emotion—real love is *action*.

LIVE IT

Jesus *commands* his disciples—and us—to love each other. To command is to give someone an order; it means telling someone to do something in an often forceful and official way.

So Jesus, when He *commands* us in this verse to love one another, isn't *suggesting* that we love one another; He is, instead, *ordering* it. As His followers, we should obey His commands whether or not we *feel* like doing so.

Therefore, if Jesus commands us to love one another, then we should love each other—including the "others" in our families—even if we don't particularly feel like it, because obedience doesn't depend on our feelings. Obedience is a choice. We can either choose to follow orders or we can choose to disregard them.

Assuming we choose to follow Christ's command to "love each other," we must keep in mind that real love is an action. To tell your mom and dad, your brother and sister that you love them is good and necessary and right. But sharing those important words—*I love you*—is only a start.

To follow the command fully means to not only *say* you love someone, it also means to *show* in action and in deed that you love the person. For example, you could tell your mom how much you

Love One Another

love her while at the same time brushing her cheek with a kiss and taking her breakfast dishes to the sink, clearing the rest of the table, and helping her load the dishwasher.

You could tell your sibling you love her while at the same time holding hands with her across the busy street and then playing with her at the park (even when your friends want you to join them at the diamond for a quick game of baseball).

You could tell your dad you love him while joining him in the garage clean-up effort (without being asked).

Granted, you may not feel like cleaning up the breakfast dishes, playing at the park, or organizing the garage, but by choosing actions that you know will bless another member of your family, you are, in effect, loving that person by your actions.

Something else to notice about Jesus' command is this: we are to love each other as *He* loved *us*.

Jesus gave His life for us. So if He wants us to love our families as He loved us, it's going to require some sacrifice.

Loving each other in your family might mean opting out of a sports season; choosing to spend time with a family member rather than with friends; getting up earlier than planned; staying up later than is comfortable; engaging in an activity that bores you (but blesses the other person); visiting a store you dislike; making a meal that isn't your favorite; eating a meal you don't enjoy; holding your tongue when you really want to lash out... Truly, the list is endless.

But the bottom line is this: Jesus commands us to love each other; He commands us to love like He loved us; and He expects that we show this love to each other by what we do.

undivided

Ask It

What is a command? How is it different than a suggestion?

Why do you think Jesus *commanded* us to love each other?

How would you describe love?

Name one way your parent/child has shown love to you.

How did Jesus love you?

What does it mean to sacrifice? Why is this important when talking about loving each other?

Give It

Things you will need for this activity:

1. A full sheet of paper for each member of your family
2. A pencil/pen for each member of your family

Hand out a blank sheet of paper to each family member and have them write their name at the top. Everyone should fold their papers and put them in a bowl.

Instruct each person to draw out a name. If you get your own name, draw again and put back your name. Don't tell anyone whose name you have.

Love One Another

On the piece of paper you've drawn from the bowl, secretly write down seven ways you are going to show your love to that person. It could be something you say, something you do, something you write, or even something you draw or create. Very small children can participate in this activity, too, but they may need a little one-on-one private coaching to help them come up with concrete ideas for showing love to the person on their paper.

Next, spend a little time during the following seven days doing each of the items on your list. You could work on one idea each day or several in one day. The choice is yours.

Finally, at the end of the week, discuss how the activity impacted each of you personally and as a family. For example, how did it affect the manner in which you showed love? How did it impact the manner in which you accepted love?

Take time to pray together after sharing.

Lesson Two:
Be Devoted to One Another

Key Verse

Be devoted to one another in love.
Honor one another above yourselves.

~Romans 12:10

Learn It

As indicated in Romans 1:1, the Apostle Paul wrote the letter to the Romans about 25 years after Jesus' death and resurrection. He was writing to a group of well-established house churches in Rome, explaining to them God's plan of salvation.

Paul's main emphasis was that people understood how to be right with God (i.e. how to be "righteous"), and that being right with God has *everything* to do with what Jesus did for us on the cross (something we believe by our faith), and *not* by what *we* do for Jesus (our actions).

undivided

However, God's love for us *should* change—radically—the way we love others. In fact, God's love for us should motivate us to "honor" others. In other words, we should desire to put others above ourselves.

Live It

In this passage, Paul tells us to "be devoted to one another" and to "honor one another," but what does that really mean?

To "be devoted" and to "honor" someone else means that we should be *doing* something—taking action. But what?

To be devoted means to be to be "steadfastly attentive to," "to give unremitting care to," "to show one's self courageous for" and "to be in constant readiness for" (from *The NAS New Testament Greek Lexicon*).

Being "steadfastly attentive" looks like turning off the TV and the iPad and the Xbox; it looks like putting down the book and the iPod and the phone; it looks like sitting together, looking one another in the eyes and *really* connecting. To be devoted to one another, then, means to unplug from other sources of pleasure and choose to "plug in" to one another.

"To give unremitting care to" one another looks like actively and continually and constantly seeking ways to adore one another. It means asking yourself, "How can I show my mom and dad that I cherish them? How can I love on my little sister? What can I do to make my brother feel connected to me? How can I show my family members that I treasure them?" To be devoted to one another, then, means to consistently look for and find ways to show interest in each family member.

Be Devoted to One Another

"To show one's self courageous for" one another means to bravely stand beside a person no matter what. It might look like defending a little brother whose feelings were hurt on the bus or advocating for your mother when she raises concerns about a movie to your friends or fielding the questions of and praying for a sibling who is struggling in her faith. To be devoted to one another, then, means to show loyalty toward a person especially when it's hard.

"To be in constant readiness for" one another means to be prepared and willing to connect at a moment's notice. It might mean entertaining a younger sibling when Mom is making dinner or running out to help an older brother rake the leaves or staying up past bedtime to talk through a pressing issue with a child. To be devoted, to one another, then, means to watch for and take advantage of those important instances of connection as they spontaneously present themselves.

In this passage, Paul is not only asking us to be devoted to one another; he is also asking us "to honor one another"… and to honor one another "above" ourselves.

To honor someone means to show preference and respect for that person; it means to defer to his or her requests. Showing honor is easiest with our parents because, of course, listening and obeying their rules shows that we have a high opinion for their authority over us.

But what does it look like to honor our siblings? And what does it look like to honor them above ourselves?

To honor a sibling looks like letting your sister play on the computer even when you really want to log on. It looks like selecting the rated G animated movie so that even the youngest brother can watch. It looks like letting your sister borrow the car and staying home for the night instead. Making these decisions requires sacrificing your own desires to place their wishes above your own and delaying your fun until later so that your siblings can have fun now.

undivided

Building devotion and honor within a family takes specific action—unselfish action usually requiring that we put a parent's or a sibling's needs above our own.

Ask It

What does it mean to be devoted to one another?

Name one way we can be devoted to each other within our family.

What does it mean to honor one another?

Name one way we can honor each other within our family.

Why is it hard to put others' needs above our own?

Has there been a time when someone in your family has put your needs ahead of their own? How did that make you feel? Share the story.

Give It

Things you will need for this activity:

1. Family calendar
2. Pencil/Pen

Be Devoted to One Another

Take a look at your family calendar for the upcoming week. Find a time each day of the week when you can spend 15-30 minutes together as a family. Each day can be different from the others: mornings, afternoons, evenings… it doesn't matter.

Discuss as a family what sacrifices need to be made to ensure that everyone is there. Make sure the sacrifices are spread evenly throughout the family so no one family member is bearing the sole burden of sacrificing their activities or time.

Each day, use those 15-30 minutes to stop and share a little more intimately together. Here are a several discussion questions to get you started, but feel free to draft your own!

1. What is/was the most exciting part of your day/week and why?
2. What are you least looking forward to this day/week and why?
3. Is there someone in your life you are thankful for and why?
4. Is there someone in your life with whom you are having problems? Why?
5. Kids: Have you honored your parents today/this week? If not, why are you struggling?
6. Kids: What has been your favorite memory as a family?
7. Parents: Have you been devoted to your children today/this week? If not, what needs to change?
8. Parents: Share with your children why you are devoted to your spouse and how you show it. Feel free to share a story from when you were dating or one from early in your marriage.

After sharing with each other, take time to pray for those areas where there are struggles and praise God for those areas that can be celebrated.

Lesson Three:
Build One Another Up

KEY VERSE

Do not let any unwholesome talk come out of your mouths,
but only what is helpful for building others up according to
their needs, that it may benefit those who listen.

~Ephesians 4:29

LEARN IT

TODAY'S KEY VERSE is taken from Ephesians, a letter originally written by Paul to Christians living in the city of Ephesus (Ephesians 1:1).

At the time, Ephesus was one of the most important cities in western Asia Minor (now modern day Turkey). The city was an intersection of major trade routes, and therefore became quite the commercial center.

Like the letter to the Romans, Ephesians discusses God's plan for salvation. However, Ephesians is also full of instructions for the church. It is clear time and again that Paul's overall prayer is that Christians "live a life worthy of the calling [they] have received" (Ephesians 4:1).

One of the ways we can live lives worthy of our calling in Christ is be sure that our words are helpful, not hurtful.

LIVE IT

Most of us know that to speak in an "unwholesome" way to each other is simply *not* kind or loving. In fact, scholars would go so far as to say that "unwholesome" talk is actually "rotten" and "useless" and even "corrupt." Our words, when they are unkind and unloving, can harm our parents, our kids, or our brothers and sisters to the point where they can pollute and poison our relationships with one another.

But we know this, right?

What is interesting about this passage is that the author doesn't *just* tell us about what kind of talk *shouldn't* be coming out of our mouths… he also tells us what kind of talk *should* be coming out of our mouths: the kind that is "helpful for building others up according to their needs."

Some people might say that this passage simply encourages us to be "nice" to each other. And while that is good and right, speaking words that "build others up" requires a little more effort than just being "nice."

Picture, for example, an old treehouse in the backyard. It has been neglected to the point where it is falling down; it needs attention. What would happen if someone just put some pretty curtains on the broken window frame or gave it a bright new paint job? Would these "nice" fixes prevent the treehouse from falling down? No.

Build One Another Up

To restore the treehouse, we would need to repair the broken cross beams, reinforce the walls, patch up the roof. Oh the "nice" touches will eventually come, but first, the foundational flaws must be addressed.

Each of us have flaws that need addressing, too, and who better to help us address those flaws than the people who love us best: our families?

For example, maybe your sister is messy and unorganized—so much so that she is having trouble keeping appointments or finding belongings or remembering promises. You could choose to yell at her for being so inconsiderate, but we've already decided that would be an unwholesome way to behave.

You could also choose to ignore her messiness, and while some people may praise you for taking this route, Ephesians 4:29 is clear: we should choose to speak in a way that builds "others up according to their needs, that it may benefit those who listen." To ignore your sister's flaw, then, would be to ignore this part of the verse, too.

What to do, then?

As a person who loves her, you could sit down with your sister over a cup of hot chocolate to gently speak with her about your observation that her disorganization seems to be affecting in a negative way not only herself but also her family and friends. And perhaps you could offer her some suggestions for how she could improve in this area of weakness. Regardless of her reaction, you could end the conversation with an affirmation of how much she means to you.

In short, "building one another up" sometimes means lovingly offering useful comments and constructive criticisms that in the long run serve to instruct, educate, improve and develop from the inside, out.

undivided

Ask It

There is an old children's rhyme that goes, "sticks and stones may break my bones, but names will never hurt me." Do you think this is true? Explain.

Share a time when you said something about which you were later sorry. Why do you think you said what you did?

Share a time when you said something that you know helped someone else. Why do you think it was helpful?

What do you think you should do when you are angry and feel like saying something hurtful?

How do you think words can point people toward Jesus?

Give It

Things you will need for this activity:

1. A pack of white paper cups (approx. 3 oz.)
2. Pen or Sharpie-style marker

Find a space in a high traffic area of your house that is flat and stable—maybe in a hallway or on a counter in the kitchen. Put a stack of the cups and the pen near this space so that they are easily accessible to everyone in the house.

Build One Another Up

Throughout the week, be conscious of using your words to encourage one another. If someone in your household, at your job, or at school says something that encourages you, take a cup and the pen and write down that person's name and the word(s) that were shared. Small children can participate with the help of older siblings or a parent.

As the week progresses and several cups have names/words written on them, begin building a tower with the cups. See how high your tower can get by the end of the week.

After seven days or so, sit down with your family and—one by one—take the cups from the tower. Share how the person's words made a difference in your week. Discuss how you can do a better job of encouraging each other.

Lesson Four:
Accept One Another

KEY VERSE

*Accept one another, then, just as Christ accepted you,
in order to bring praise to God.*

~Romans 15:7

LEARN IT

CONFLICT HAPPENS. Even in the best of relationships, there may be moments of disagreement and discord, argument and misunderstanding.

As mentioned before, Paul's letter to the Romans emphasizes how to be right with God. In chapters 14-15, Paul's teaching gets specific as he addresses how we should behave when we find ourselves having opinions that are different than those of our fellow brothers and sisters in Christ.

undivided

The bottom line is this: we have *all* sinned; we *all* sometimes struggle to obey God; and yet, as Christians, we are *all* accepted by God the Father because of what Jesus did for us on the cross.

Because we are all accepted by God through the saving work of Jesus Christ, we should work hard to lovingly accept one another in spite of disagreements and discord, arguments and misunderstandings—especially within our families. When we do, God gets the praise!

Live It

Have you ever apologized to your brother NOT because you regretted hurting him, but because your parents told you to do it? And then, when you finally uttered the words "I'm sorry," they came out in a less-than-kind-and-loving tone?

It's not enough to say the "right" words. No. What we think in our minds and believe in our hearts must match what comes out of our mouths. Anything less disappoints God.

Because here's the thing: when *we* do something that grieves God's heart, and when we go to Him with genuine sorrow for what we did, He absolutely forgives us 100% of the time. He harbors NO ill will toward us. He "accepts" us because of who Jesus is and what Jesus did on the cross. He gives us access to His heart and takes us back unto Himself in friendship.

Because He forgives *us* and accepts *us* back into real relationship with Him *every single time,* He expects us to do that for *others*—especially our brothers and sisters and parents!

So when your little sister breaks into your room and accidentally ruins one of your toys? Or when your big brother forgets that he had plans with you and goes off with his friends instead? Or when your dad yelled at you a little too loudly and abruptly when you interrupted him? Or when your mom neglected to tell you that practice had been changed and so you missed it? In every single one of these circumstances and more, you are to "accept one another." Not because you feel like it (because really, you might NOT feel like it at first), but because this is what Jesus does for you. And therefore, He expects us to do it for each other.

It's important to know, too, that to "accept one another" is deeper than just tolerating the presence of a family member or keeping the peace with him/her by avoidance.

Instead, it means to receive them back into your heart with kindness and to take them once again by the hand as companions with whom you desire to spend time.

Is this easy? No. Sometimes the hurt inflicted upon us by those closest to us is horribly painful simply because it came from those who know us most intimately. And so our human response is to back away and to hold them at a distance.

But consider this: God loves us more intimately than anyone. He knows our innermost thoughts and feelings and sins. We hurt Him to the core and even though we do not deserve it, He accepts us and reaffirms us and draws us closer to Him each time after we mess up.

And so we must do the same with our brothers and sisters and parents; we must accept one another even after we hurt one another, because that is what Christ does for us.

When we accept one another, other people will see, and they will speak highly of our God.

Isn't it amazing to think that the way we treat our family members can serve to help other people see our God more clearly?

ASK IT

Have you ever told someone in your family you were "sorry" but didn't really mean it? Why do you think it was so hard to apologize?

divided

What do you think it means when God says we should "accept" one another?

Share with each other a time when you have felt hurt or sad by the words or actions of someone else.

Did that person ever apologize? If not, how did that make you feel?

Do you think you hurt God with your words or actions? If so, how?

What did God do to show us that He accepts us no matter how many times we hurt Him?

What can we do to show God how much we love Him for accepting us?

GIVE IT

Things you will need for this activity:

1. One, large cross cut out of construction paper or cardboard (at least 1-2 feet high)
2. Heart-shaped paper cutouts for each person in your family
3. Pen/pencil
4. Glue or push pins

Accept One Another

Sit around a table or in a circle on the floor. Place the cross in the center of your circle.

Give a paper heart to each individual along with a pen or pencil.

Have each person write on their heart something about themselves that they know God would like them to change. Try not to talk during this time so everyone has time for introspection. If children are having a hard time coming up with ideas, brainstorm possibilities together. Make sure everyone has completed this task before moving to the next step.

Once everyone is finished, go around the table and talk about what you have written and why you feel God wants you to change that part of your life. After each person finishes talking, glue or pin your heart to the cross as a way of recognizing that in spite of this issue, God accepts you and forgives you. Use the cross as a centerpiece on your kitchen table for a week and see if it sparks further conversation.

Lesson Five:
Instruct One Another

KEY VERSE

I myself am convinced, my brothers and sisters, that you yourselves are full of goodness, filled with knowledge and competent to instruct one another.

~Romans 15:14

LEARN IT

PAUL'S LETTER TO THE ROMANS is full of great wisdom for us in terms of how we can live for one another as this is the third verse we are choosing to study from Romans!

In Romans 15:13, the passage just before our key verse, Paul prays that we might "overflow with hope by the power of the Holy Spirit." This short, powerful prayer is a great reminder that any hope, goodness, knowledge or spiritual competence we have comes from God through the power of His Holy Spirit.

undivided

It is not surprising, then, that Paul suggests that we can and should be a gift to one another by teaching each other. Being in relationship with others means we can give one another valuable instruction.

For example, has anyone ever told you something that ended up being very helpful? Has someone ever told you something that maybe protected you from something dangerous?

Even though it may sometimes be difficult to both give and receive instruction, God gifts us with spiritual knowledge and competence so that we, in turn, may teach others... beginning with those in our families.

LIVE IT

Let's face it: sometimes, it's hard to receive instruction from anyone—especially from our siblings or parents—because we simply feel like we have everything under control and that we don't need to hear wisdom or truth or teaching from someone else.

And sometimes, it's even harder to give instruction to others for a variety of reasons such as feeling like we're intruding or as if the person we're trying to speak to is unwilling to receive it.

However, none of this gets us off the hook. Scripture is clear: we who are "full of goodness and filled with knowledge" and competence are supposed to "instruct one another."

What does this look like in a family?

If you see your sister making unwise decisions at school, it means praying for the words God would have you to share with her... words that would speak to her heart and situation; words that would help open her eyes to the wrong choices she is making. And then it means making time to sit down with her, maybe over ice cream, to share with her the observations you have about what has been going on at school.

Instruct One Another

As sons and daughters, it means that we should be ready to receive instruction from our parents, no matter how much we think we already know. The fact is that Mom and Dad have already been our age, and so they know a thing or two about what we are facing. Sometimes they can see our plight more clearly, and therefore we need to be open to hearing their words of wisdom even if we don't feel like it. So when they ask to sit down with us to share with us their observations, there should be no eye-rolling or heavy sighing. Instead, we should listen well.

God has blessed us with family members—people who see us at our best and at our worst; people who see us at morning, noon and night; people who love us deeply through the good and the bad—to speak to us words of truth and instruction, reprimand and encouragement, warning and information. Because we know one another so well, God wants us to be willing to take the time to counsel each other as He presents opportunities.

Our job, then, in family, is to be alert for teachable moments—moments where God would have us to listen to and/or give instruction.

It is important to note that parents can (and should) learn from their children, that older siblings can (and should) learn from each other, and that all instruction exchanged can (and should) be filled with kindness.

Bottom line: God created the family not just so we'd have warm cozy places to lay our heads and good times eating together around the table. No. He created the family as a way to impart instruction—His instruction—in a relationally kind, loving and safe environment.

undivided

Ask It

When is the last time someone told you something that ended up being very helpful? At first, were you excited to hear that person share those words with you? If not, what eventually made you take that person's advice?

How do you think we should share information that a person may not want to hear?

Why does God desire that we instruct one another?

Why is it hard to be corrected or have someone point out that you are wrong?

Kids: What are areas in your life about which you wish your parents would talk with you more?

Parents: How do you think your children can instruct or "correct" you without showing disrespect?

Give It

Things you will need for this activity:

1. Model car, airplane, boat, etc. that is cheap and easy to put together

Instruct One Another

You will be building a model car, airplane, etc. as a family. Open up the box, spread out all the parts, and give one person the directions.

The person with the directions must instruct the family through the first step without showing any pictures or letting them read the instruction sheet themselves.

Once the first step is complete, the person with the directions should pass them to the person on his/her right. The person who now has the directions should talk the family through step two. Continue this pattern until the model is complete.

The key point to this activity is to be mindful of how you can best give instruction without your family getting upset or frustrated in the process. Everyone should be aware of the tone they are using when they communicate with each other. Feel free to stop the activity if the situation feels too tense or if anyone is getting frustrated. Talk out why there is frustration and then resume the activity.

Lesson Six:
Serve One Another

KEY VERSE

You, my brothers and sisters, were called to be free.
But do not use your freedom to indulge the flesh rather,
serve one another humbly in love.

~Galatians 5:13

LEARN IT

WITH TODAY'S KEY VERSE, we again look at a letter from Paul—this time a letter addressed to the churches in Galatia (likely modern day Turkey).

Much of Galatians teaches the church to be careful about believing things that weren't true about the gospel (the good news that God saves us and we don't save ourselves). In essence, Paul wanted the people—both then and now—to remember that we are saved by grace, through faith in Jesus, and not by anything that we do. Our faith in Jesus and His work on the cross is what saves us. Period. Nothing more and nothing less.

And when we believe in Christ—when we become Christians—we are born into a new family, the church. As people who follow Jesus, and therefore as people motivated by God's love, we should be moved to take care not only of our own needs, but also of the needs of others—especially fellow believers.

In Paul's words, we are to "serve one another humbly in love," *not* because we have to, but because we *want* to!

LIVE IT

Serving others does not come naturally. Instead, what comes naturally is to serve ourselves. We tend to think of our needs and wants first before thinking at all about how we could serve someone else.

Some of our needs include nourishment and sleep, and for those needs, we *can* depend upon our feelings to trigger appropriate responses. For example, if you're feeling hungry or thirsty, it's probably a good idea to stop what you're doing to get something to eat or drink; if you're feeling tired, perhaps you should take a nap or get to bed earlier. In these cases, feelings prompt good and appropriate responses.

However, there are other times—many other times—when feelings prompt ungodly desires in us. Like when your little sister knocks over your Lego masterpiece or your dad eats the last donut; when your mom borrows the shoes you were going to wear today or your brother stays in the shower too long making it impossible for you to get ready on time. It's in these situations that we need to be careful about going where our feelings want to take us.

Serve One Another

For example, if we were to "indulge the flesh," as Paul mentions, then we might yell ugly words or hit or stomp around or refuse to share, all which are sinful behaviors. So, even though the actions of our family members make us *feel* like sinning, Paul commands us NOT to give in to those feelings.

Instead, we should practice what doesn't come so naturally; we should "serve one another humbly in love."

Wow is this hard!

It might mean taking the time to sit next to your crushed Lego masterpiece with your little sister to calmly explain your disappointment, to lovingly extend your forgiveness to her, and to patiently help her make her very own masterpiece.

It might mean going without breakfast or telling your mom how pretty she looks in your shoes or foregoing your morning shower.

None of these responses come naturally, but all of them display a servant's heart willing to choose respectful, loving behavior over our more typical sin-filled choices.

Make no mistake about it: we are sinful people, and our first wish is usually to please ourselves rather than to defer to the needs and feelings and desires of someone else.

Therefore, Paul urges us to be conscious of ways we can work for (or serve) the good of others. To do this requires thinking less about ourselves and what we need/want and more (much more!) about what others need/want.

Bottom line? We always have a choice… are we going to choose to please ourselves or are we going to seek ways to serve our family members in love?

Ask It

Paul teaches that we are saved by God's grace and mercy. What do you think life would be like if we always had to earn God's salvation through work or rules?

Why do you think God wants us to be free to love or reject Him?

Define selfishness.

Who is our biggest obstacle to serving others? Why do you think it's hard to put others above ourselves?

Most often, missionaries follow their calling from God to serve others in different countries. If you were going to be a missionary, where would you go to serve others? How would you serve others there?

What is one small way you can serve someone else this week?

Give It

Things you will need for this activity:

1. Varies depending on the act of service

Serve One Another

As a family, think of another person or perhaps a family that needs a helping hand. It could be a neighbor, a relative, someone from work or a family from church. If you can't think of anyone, call your church to see if there are any requests or ask to be put on a list to help should someone call.

Next, determine how your family can best serve that individual or family. It may be as simple as cleaning up a yard or making a meal; or it may be more continuous in nature like picking up a child each day from an activity after school because the family is without transportation.

Whatever the need, try to make sure your entire family is incorporated into the serving process. Even younger kids can help with simple tasks such as pouring ingredients into a bowl to help make a meal or picking up sticks in the yard or even playing with the other children while mom and dad talk to the parents.

Discuss throughout this time of serving what is difficult and what comes easily. Be honest with each other. God knows your heart and He has put your family together specifically to encourage you through your struggles.

Lesson Seven:
Carry One Another's Burdens

KEY VERSE

Carry each other's burdens, and in this way you will fulfill the law of Christ.

~Galatians 6:2

LEARN IT

HAVE YOU EVER HAD TO CARRY something heavy all by yourself? As a part of God's family, the church, we should never have to carry something heavy without help.

Similar to the previous lesson, today's key verse—a command to "carry each other's burdens" from Paul's letter to the Galatians—reminds us that we don't follow Jesus alone.

Carrying something with someone else's assistance is always easier! And as a part of God's family, the church, we should never have to carry something heavy without help. Likewise, we are to help carry each other's "burdens" in our "earthly" families, as well.

LIVE IT

If we are going to "carry each other's burdens" in such a way that we will "fulfill the law of Christ," then we need to understand the term "burden."

A burden is something that is hard to manage like a bulky load or a heavy weight.

For example, our two-year-old struggled just this morning to carry a basket of laundry up the stairs in our house. The basket weighed her down so much that she was unable to complete her climb. I came alongside her, lifted one side of the basket, and—just like that—we were able to finish the job… *together.*

In this illustration, the weighty laundry basket was too much for our girl to handle; however, with someone to help carry the "burden," she was able to move forward. This is what it looks like when we carry "each other's burdens."

In family, there will be times when a person will enter a season where there is simply too much to bear, and without help, that person will be unable to move forward. But, if we step in to "carry each other's burdens," we can help each other to progress.

Sometimes, the burdens we help each other carry in family are obvious like in the laundry basket story above. Perhaps Mom has gone back to school and everyone else in the family needs to pitch in to prepare meals and maintain family commitments in order to give her time to complete homework assignments. Or maybe it's dance recital time for a sister, and because she has extra rehearsals, her brother offers to do the dishes even though it's not his turn.

Carry One Another's Burdens

There could also be times when a burden seemingly appears from nowhere, when test results indicate that a brother is very sick, for example, and in order to help the whole family, dad might take on another job to help pay medical bills, mom might quit her part time job to take the brother to and from doctor appointments, and older siblings might take over the care of younger children—all of this to help "carry the burden" caused by the unforeseen illness.

But there are other times when the burdens we help each other carry aren't necessarily physical in nature. Someone might have a faith crisis, and we can come alongside him to study scripture in order to answer any questions he might have or to cover the family member in prayer.

Someone might experience mental anguish during a thunderstorm, and to help her through the night, her older brother might pull a sleeping bag into her room for comfort and assurance.

Someone might encounter an incredibly difficult life decision—perhaps a career change, a university choice, a marriage proposal—and he needs hours of time with mom and dad to help him weigh all of his options.

Someone might need help sharing because whenever she has a friend over she finds it really, really hard to let others play with her toys, and therefore she is sad because no one wants to play with her. She needs the wisdom of her older sister who might carve out some special time in her schedule to play with her and to talk to her about what it means to be a good friend.

In every one of these scenarios, a family member comes alongside another family member to relieve a burden and in so doing, the family is strengthened.

But also, the cause of Christ is strengthened, too.

Because when people see the kind of love that selflessly causes family members to carry the burdens of siblings and parents and children, they understand that it is a special kind of love, indeed.

undivided

And when others see this special kind of love in your family, it may give you the opportunity to share the story of Jesus. Because after all, it is His love that makes the burden-carrying love possible.

Ask It

What is a burden?

Describe a time in your life when you felt a burden that was too heavy to carry all by yourself. Did someone help you through that time? How did that feel?

Do you think it is easier or harder to help carry the burdens of your family versus your friends? Why do you think that is?

Do you have a current burden in your life? Share with your family what that burden is and discuss how they can help you carry it.

Give It

Things you will need for this activity:

1. Backpack
2. 20 large rocks (as large as your fist)
3. If you can't find large rocks, get a bag of landscaping rocks

This week you are going to go for a family hike. Choose your favorite forrest, park, or—if it is too cold outside—indoor area where your entire family can walk and talk throughout this activity.

Carry One Another's Burdens

When you arrive at your chosen location, take out the backpack and have someone volunteer to put it on first. (Don't worry, everyone will carry the backpack!) Have the rest of the family begin loading up the backpack with rocks. Fill it as full as you can, but not so much you can't carry it. These rocks represent your burdens.

Now, go on your hike together as a family. As you are walking, share with each other things in your life that tend to weigh you down. Encourage one another and see if there are ways you can share in each other's burdens.

After awhile, someone in the family should volunteer to carry the backpack and relieve the "burden" of the family member bearing the entire weight of this activity. Continue sharing the backpack with each other along your hike. Remember, smaller members of the family may not be able to carry it at all. This may require the whole family to assist in bearing the weight of the backpack by lifting up on the bottom so the child can move forward. Take this opportunity to discuss how not all family members can share equally in bearing each other's burdens.

Work as a team (and a family!) until your hike is complete. Then reward yourself with some ice cream on the way home and discuss what you learned!

Lesson Eight:
Encourage One Another

KEY VERSE

*Therefore encourage one another and build each other up,
just as in fact you are doing.*

~1 Thessalonians 5:11

LEARN IT

PAUL WROTE THE LETTER TO THE THESSALONIANS to encourage the church—a church he, Silas and Timothy started in the city of Thessalonica (see Acts 17:1-9). The church consisted of both Jewish and Gentile Christians—all of them believers who had placed their faith in Jesus as Savior.

Unfortunately, intense persecution forced the men to get out of Thessalonica shortly after starting the church (Acts 17:10), leaving the new Christians without a lot of support. Therefore, Paul writes to the Thessalonian believers to encourage them, and he challenges them to "build each other up" in Christ, just as they had been doing all along.

Similarly, it is important for us in our families to "encourage one another and build each other up" so that we can help each other to continue growing in Christ, too.

LIVE IT

What's interesting about 1 Thessalonians 5:11 is that Paul is telling the people to do something that they are, in fact, already doing!

That's like your baseball coach saying, "Choke up on the bat and keep your eye on the ball, *like you've been doing for the last ten games.*"

Or like your piano teacher saying, "Curve your fingers and sit up straight on the bench, *like you've been doing for the last four years of lessons.*"

And maybe your mom and dad have said something similar, too, like, "Speak kindly to your sister, especially in the mornings as you know mornings aren't her most agreeable times. *You've already been doing this, I know, but please continue!*"

Why in the world would Paul tell the Thessalonians to keep encouraging one another and building each other up if they're already doing it? For the same reason coaches and teachers and parents remind us to keep doing the good things that we're already doing: those good behaviors are producing good results, so we need to keep doing them.

We need to remember not to forget!

For example, if you hit the ball out of the park every time you remember to choke up on the bat, then certainly, choking up on the bat would be a good thing to keep doing.

Encourage One Another

And if you're able to play beautiful music with curved fingers and proper posture, then of course your teacher will want you to keep those specifics in mind when sitting down at the piano.

Similar reminders work just as well in our families: if mornings go smoothly especially when you remember to speak kindly to your sister, then it is worth reminding you to use gentle words.

So it is good that Paul lovingly reminds the people to keep encouraging one another and building each other up even though it's something they're already doing well.

And it's a great reminder for us, too, that growing stronger in the faith—no matter what we're trying to improve—takes time, effort and focus. We must keep on growing.

That said, how can we get even better at encouraging each other and building each other up in our families? Awareness.

Paul helped the Thessalonians to be aware of what it was they were already doing well, and he told them to keep doing it.

In order to do the same thing in our families, let's think about the definitions of "encourage" and "building up."

While we typically think of encouragement as something we do that cheers up or motivates someone, the word here means that and more. For example, if we are hiking in the woods and we see that someone is veering off the correct path, we might "encourage" him to join us again on the right trail.

Similarly, taking the time to intentionally encourage a family member might mean cheering him up when he didn't make the team, motivating her to try the song again after struggling with it at rehearsal, or inspiring him to have a potentially difficult discussion with a heartbroken friend.

"To build up" was a term originally used when referring to the construction of a building. In this case, Paul likely meant the phrase as an analogy to the "construction" of a person's character.

undivided

People of Christian character are noted for continuous growth in such areas as love, joy, peace, patience, kindness, goodness, faithfulness, gentleness and self-control (see Galatians 5:22-23).

So, in short, encouraging or "building up" our family members means doing whatever we can to help one another develop deeper Christian virtues.

ASK IT

What happens when you encourage someone to keep doing something they are already doing? Why is this important?

What do you think would happen if you never mentioned someone's positive attributes and only focused on the negative ones? If someone did that to you, how would you feel?

Is there something you have done over the past year or two that has brought you to a deeper understanding of your faith in Christ? If so, share it with others (Attention family members: this is where you encourage one another!!!)

Other than someone sitting in the room, who has been the most encouraging to you in your lifetime? Share what they have done to be encouraging.

Who do you feel you have done a good job encouraging lately? Is there anyone you would like to encourage better? Why don't you think you have been encouraging to that person?

Give It

Things you will need for this activity:

1. One tennis ball

Sit on the floor in a circle. One person will start the activity. S/he will be the "server."

The server throws/rolls the ball to a person in the circle. That person is the "receiver." The server must then start a sentence with the first prompt (below) and finish the sentence.

After the server has completed his/her sentence, the receiver now becomes the server and must "serve" the ball to the next person. Make sure each prompt is used by multiple people before moving on to the next one.

This activity may get silly at times, but remember there is often truth being shared even amidst the silliness. Most of all, be encouraging to one another!!

Prompts

1. I love it when you…

2. You have probably never heard me say this about you, but I…

3. You may not know this, but one time you made my day when you…

4. Sing the following to the person: "You are my sunshine, my only sunshine, you make me happy, when…"

5. There are three things that I would never change about you, they are…

Lesson Nine:
Be at Peace with One Another

KEY VERSE

Salt is good, but if it loses its saltiness, how can you make it salty again?
Have salt among yourselves, and be at peace with each other.

~Mark 9:50

LEARN IT

THE NEW TESTAMENT BEGINS with four books: the Gospels of Matthew, Mark, Luke and John.

Greek in origin, the word "gospel" is translated as "good news." Thus, the Gospels are literally God's "good news," which is all about Jesus. The Gospels tell us who Jesus is, what He taught, and how He lived, died and came to life again.

Our key verse today comes from the Gospel of Mark which was written by John Mark (a good friend of Peter, one of Jesus' disciples), and most likely addressed to a group of Gentile Christians living in the city of Rome.

undivided

Mark 9:50 quotes Jesus who encourages His followers to "be at peace with each other."

LIVE IT

"Have salt among yourselves, and be at peace with each other."

What?

Does this mean we should all stock up on our salt shakers? As funny as that image is, it wasn't really the point of what Jesus was teaching.

To get the point of the message, we need to think about salt. Why did Jesus say Christians should "have salt among yourselves?"

One theory is that because salt is white, it could symbolize purity and cleanliness and how we are supposed to be holy and separate to do the work of God.

Also, most people like to add salt to particularly bland dishes such as eggs or potatoes because it makes them more tasty. Like the salt adds flavor to food, we Christians are to add a sort of "divine seasoning" to the world.

Furthermore, consuming a lot of salt makes us thirsty, so we Christians are to live in such a way as to make people "thirsty" for Christ.

Salt is also a preservative; it stops decay. Because many of the disciples were fishermen, they would have understood and appreciated this very important function of salt. Why? Unlike us, they didn't have refrigeration! As soon as they pulled their fish onto the boat, they would have packed their catch with salt or else it would have quickly spoiled and rotted. "Salty" Christians, then, act as a kind of preservative in this corrupt world, preventing the disease of sin to rot, destroy and decay lives.

So... now that we understand a little better what Jesus meant when He said we should "have salt among" ourselves, it's a little more clear why He wants us to be at peace with each other. Because here's the thing: when we aren't at peace with one another, then we begin to lose the "saltiness" of our faith.

When we aren't at peace with our parents or our siblings, our ability to affect the world with the message of Jesus is hindered, and this is why He wants us to be at peace within our families.

Maintaining peace in your family might mean choosing to take out the trash even though it's not your turn; holding your tongue when you'd really, *really* like to lash out in anger; speaking kind words even in the wake of meanspirited phrases uttered to annoy or irritate you; deciding to be friendly and helpful even when a sibling is completely inconsiderate and selfish.

Regaining peace in your family might mean asking forgiveness for wrongly accusing a child of not doing his chores; apologizing for harsh words uttered in anger; expressing regret for a poor decision.

Both regaining and maintaining peace in your family is necessary to ensure that your family has "salt among yourselves"—a requirement for being people who effectively share the good news of Jesus with the world.

ASK IT

Why did Jesus compare our lives to salt?

If salt can be used as a preservative, what do you think we should be "preserving"? What do you think your friends would say about this?

Peace can be a tricky word to define. How would you define it?

Both Christians and unbelievers talk about wanting peace. Is there a difference in the type of peace we are seeking? Why do you think it is so hard to have peace in this world?

undivided

When you are fighting with someone in your family, do you feel peaceful inside? Do you think others in your household feel peaceful?

Why do you think it is hard to admit when you're wrong? Does it take you a long or short time to admit your faults? Why do you think that is?

Give It

Things you will need for this activity:

1. Two tall drinking glasses
2. Two uncooked eggs
3. Table salt

In this activity, you are going to see how important salt is to raising up God's message of salvation for the world to see. For this easy experiment, the egg represents the Good News of Jesus Christ, the glasses of water are the world, and the salt is you!

Fill both glasses with tap water equally about ¾ of the way full. In one glass, add 4 heaping tablespoons of salt and stir until fully dissolved.

Now the moment of truth! Put one egg in each glass and see what happens. The glass with the salt in it should make the egg float to the top while the other egg sinks to the bottom.

This will be fun for the smaller kids in the household. For the older kids, they may want to experiment with how much salt is needed for the egg to float or add in tap water to the salty water to see if the egg will sink.

Just keep in mind the analogy that in order for the Good News of Jesus Christ to rise to the top in our lives, we must be *salt*!

Lesson Ten:
Rejoice with One Another

Key Verse

*If one part suffers, every part suffers with it; if one
part is honored, every part rejoices with it.*

~1 Corinthians 12:26

Learn It

CONSIDERED DURING PAUL'S TIME as one of the most important
cities in Greece, Corinth thrived commercially, as a crossroads for
both travelers and traders; culturally, as a place to discuss current
trends in philosophy and wisdom; and religiously, as a location where
temples housed idols of false gods to worship.

Thankfully, the city of Corinth had a Christian church, but it was
kind of a mess! In fact, the reason the Apostle Paul wrote to the church
in Corinth was to try to clear up some of its sin, disagreements and
wrong beliefs.

undivided

For most of 1 Corinthians 12, Paul describes how God's family—His church—is like one body with many parts. He reminds the Corinthian Christians that when "one part suffers, every part suffers with it" and that "if one part is honored, every part rejoices."

It is the same within our families!

LIVE IT

If you fall and break your leg, it will affect your entire body. For example, your arms will have to hold onto crutches in order to help you walk on only one leg. Your mind will have to be extra careful to avoid any pitfalls that may cause you to injure the already broken area. Your good leg will have to work extra hard to hold up the rest of your body. In short, when one part of your body suffers, every part of your body is affected.

Similarly, when one member of your family suffers, everyone is affected as well. If Dad is sick and in bed for a week, everyone in the family must rally together to make sure Dad's responsibilities are covered and to nurse him back to health.

If a brother and a sister are fighting, everyone in the family experiences distress from the division.

If a grandparent dies, everyone in the family rearranges their schedules to make sure that together they can properly prepare for the funeral ceremony and family visits.

No matter what the affliction (physical, mental, emotional, material) and no matter who is touched (young child, older sibling, mom, dad, college student, baby)—every part of the family shares in the suffering.

And that is good, because grief and heartache and pain experienced together can be shared.

Rejoice with One Another

It should follow, then, that whenever a part of the family is honored, the whole family will rejoice. This can be especially difficult when sibling rivalry enters the scene. Perhaps two sisters play in the same softball league and one is chosen for the all-star team, but the other isn't. As painful as that is (and it is painful!), the two sisters can maintain true peace and harmony with one another if together they grieve the loss of the all-star experience for the one sister and together they rejoice for the opportunity of the all-star experience for the other sister.

Oftentimes, jealousy creeps into families—especially wreaking havoc on sibling relationships—and when left unaddressed, it prevents individual family members from joining together… to both "suffer" together and "rejoice" together.

When jealousy enters the fold, it should be greeted and acknowledged for what it is: a personal discontentment and resentfulness caused by something good that happens to someone else (whether it be an ability, a hardearned achievement, material possessions, etc.).

Of course we are not to remain in a state of jealousy. Instead, we are to turn from it, replacing envy with gratitude for what we do have, and in this case, replacing the unhappiness with genuine expression of joy for the other person.

It is not easy, and sometimes we won't *feel* like rejoicing for another family member who has received an honor that we wanted… but, as we've learned earlier in this devotional, we cannot always depend on our feelings to lead us to correct behavior. Instead, we can lean once again on the truth of scripture which tells us that "if one part is honored, then every part rejoices with it."

And this is also good, because honor and joy and excitement that is shared will double and triple and quadruple the rejoicing!

ASK IT

Do you get jealous easily? If so, why do you think you get jealous rather than share in the happiness with someone else?

Have you ever prayed for God to take away your jealousy? If so, share with everyone what happened after you prayed. Do you still struggle or did your jealousy go away?

Give an example when someone in your family suffered and describe how it affected you and everyone else. What would you change about the situation?

Give an example when someone in your family had great success and describe how it affected you and everyone else. Is there anything you would change about your reaction to the situation?

Is it harder to share in a family member's success or their suffering? Does it depend on the family member? If so, why do you think that is?

GIVE IT

Things you will need for this activity:

1. Recipes for each family member

Rejoice with One Another

Find an evening when everyone is home for dinner. For this activity, every family member is going to cook a portion of the family dinner. You can either be organized and assign courses to each other (e.g. salad, side dish, entree, dessert, etc.) or just have fun with it and let everyone choose their favorite dish (just be aware that everyone may be eating 5-6 different desserts for dinner!)

There are three rules for this activity that everyone must follow:

1. Each family member gets to choose what they want to cook

2. Each family member must eat at least a small portion of everything that has been cooked for this meal

3. There are no "do-overs." If Johnny burns the mac-n-cheese, everyone must "suffer" and eat some of the burnt mac-n-cheese.

For smaller children, you may want to pair them up with mom, dad or an older sibling for this activity.

Remember this week's theme as you sit down to eat together. Are you "suffering" or "rejoicing" through this meal together? Discuss why you think it is important to have shared experiences, good or bad, together as a family.

If the dinner turns out great, make it a new family tradition!

Lesson Eleven:
Pray for One Another

KEY VERSE

Therefore confess your sins to each other and pray for each other so that you may be healed. The prayer of a righteous person is powerful and effective.

~James 5:16

LEARN IT

TODAY'S KEY VERSE COMES FROM a letter written by James, a man most scholars believe was one of Jesus' brothers mentioned in Matthew 13:55. As leader of the Jerusalem church at the time, James wrote to encourage and teach fellow Christians who, after Stephen's death (Acts 7:54-60), had scattered far from their homes.

James knew that some people say they have faith in Jesus but don't act like it; he also knew that actions and behavior show what people really believe. Therefore, James instructed Christians how to live out their faith in a practical way.

One way to live faith in a real way is to pray for one another. It is easy to pray for what *we* want or need, but as Christians, we are *also* supposed to pray for the needs of others.

LIVE IT

So often when we approach God in prayer, we treat Him like a vending machine. We stand before Him thinking that if we say just the right thing for exactly the right amount of time with the proper attitude, then He will give us whatever we desire. And if we're honest, those prayers are usually focused on our own needs and desires rather than on anyone else's needs and desires.

So when James tells us to pray for one another, he means for us to do this selflessly, focused completely on the other person and with no interest in getting anything in return for ourselves.

Furthermore, these verses tell us that *first*, we are to hear the confessed sins of the other person; and *then*, we are to pray for that person so that he or she may be healed.

This could get a little awkward because these verses encourage us to confess our sins to each other!

So Mom might acknowledge the bitter words she spoke at grandma last night by telling Dad the whole story, and as she confesses her sin, Dad might be making mental notes about ways he can pray for Mom. If Dad's relationship is right with God (or if he is "righteous"), then when he prays for Mom, his prayer will be "powerful and effective," bringing "healing" for Mom.

Maybe your brother is tormented by something he did to wrong a friend. You can see that he is upset, and when you ask him about it, he reveals what he did to hurt the friend. As he talks about what happened, you recognize the whole exchange as a confession. As soon as your brother finishes talking, you offer to pray for him. As a person whose relationship is right with God ("righteous"), your prayers will be "powerful and effective" and they will bring healing to your sibling.

Can you imagine the kind of world we could be living in if fellow believers could go to one another, confess their sins, pray for each other, and bring about powerful and effective healing?

ASK IT

What is sin? What is the result of sin? (You may want to read Galatians 5:19-21 and Isaiah 59:2 to add depth and understanding to these questions.)

What is prayer? Why is it important to pray? Do you believe prayer works? Why or why not?

Do you pray regularly? If not, what keeps you from prayer?

For whom do you pray most often? In the verse for this lesson, for whom does it say we should pray? Why do you think James says this?

Do you have trouble admitting to yourself that you were wrong (sinful)? What about to others?

un**divided**

What keeps you from sharing your sins and struggles with your family? Is there something that can change that will allow you to share more readily your sins and shortcomings with your family? Talk about how you can better trust each other with these confessions.

Give It

Things you will need for this activity:

1. Candle/matches
2. Bowl of water
3. Scrap pieces of paper
4. Pencil or pen

Confessing sins to each other is hard—very hard. Pride so often gets in the way.

It is important for this activity that everyone feels safe to share with each other. If your family is going to be vulnerable with each other, there needs to be mutual trust.

In the middle of the room or on a table, light a candle. Place the bowl of water right next to it and the scraps of paper with the pen next to the bowl.

Go around the room and confess something you did or said that you know did not please God. If possible, think of a circumstance that involves your family, but if you can't think of any, you can talk about a circumstance outside your family.

Once you have confessed, the person whom you offended should take a piece of paper and write, "I forgive you" on the paper and hand it back to the person.

Pray for One Another

Go around the table until everyone has completed a confession and has a piece of paper.

Now that you have confessed to one another, you can take your sins to God who will, by His mercy and grace, extinguish them from His memory forever (Hebrews 8:12).

Next, take your piece of paper and hold it over the candle until it catches fire. After it has burned a little bit, place it in the bowl of water to extinguish the flame. Be careful not to burn your fingers!

Finally, pray for each other. You can either go around the table and pray for those who confessed to you, or have a parent pray for each person.

Lesson Twelve:
Forgive One Another

Key Verse

*Be kind and compassionate to one another, forgiving each other,
just as in Christ God forgave you.*

~Ephesians 4:32

Learn It

As mentioned in Lesson 3, the Apostle Paul wrote the letter to the Ephesians to remind them how Christians are saved and to instruct them further how members within God's family—the church—should live.

Like the Ephesians, we need such reminders, too, because even though we as Christians believe in and follow Jesus, we still do things we shouldn't; we still sin. Thankfully, because of the work of His Son Jesus Christ on the cross, God forgives us who trust in Him.

undivided

And, just as God has forgiven us, we need to learn to forgive one another. We all fall short of being perfect, and therefore we all need forgiveness in our relationships with one another.

LIVE IT

In this passage, we aren't just to be kind and compassionate and forgiving to each other, we are to do these things *just like Jesus did them for us.*

Whoa.

Jesus loved us so much that He came here to willingly die a terrible death so that we could live in Heaven with Him forever. We are to be *that* loving to *not only* strangers, but also to our families. In other words, we are supposed to love our parents just like *Jesus* loved *us;* we are supposed to love our brothers and sisters just like *Jesus* loved *us.*

It is important to note that when Jesus forgave us, He didn't ask that we act in a special way or pay a certain price or say a specific prayer; His gift of forgiveness had no strings attached. In fact, there is absolutely nothing we can do to earn His forgiveness because He gives it freely to us.

And that is how you are to forgive your little sister when she destroys your brand new phone by dropping it into the toilet.

It is how you are to forgive your older brother after he deleted the homework assignment you had on the computer.

It is how you are to forgive your mom who scheduled great-grandma's birthday celebration on the same weekend as prom.

It is how you are to forgive your dad who said he'd be able to take you to the movies but can't now because he has to work.

It is how you are to forgive your parents for embarrassing you in front of your friends… your brother for speaking to you in an ugly tone of voice… your sister for ruining your favorite blouse… your mom for sharing your secret with your friend's mom.

The list of offenses could go on and on. Thankfully, for Christians, Jesus Christ graciously meets each repentant believer's offense with forgiveness.

And therefore, we are called to forgive each other, too; and, like Jesus did for us, we are to forgive expecting nothing in return. We extend forgiveness NOT because anyone is worthy of it, but because our God forgave us and asked for nothing in return either.

ASK IT

What is the difference between forgiveness and accepting an apology?

Have you ever been forgiven for something you did wrong or for something about which you were ashamed? How did it make you feel when that person forgave you?

Is it easier or harder to forgive family? Why?

Why is God's forgiveness so important in our lives? What can we learn from the fact that He forgave us before we were even born?

Why do you think God wants nothing for His forgiveness except our love and devotion?

Is there someone in your life that you need to forgive? If so, why have you not done so yet? Can anyone in your family help? Please share.

Give It

Things you will need for this activity:

1. Big bowl of popcorn (maybe two big bowls depending on the size of your family!)
2. Smaller empty bowls for each family member
3. Movie

It can be difficult to forgive someone—especially if someone offends you over and over again. As humans, we want to know when enough is enough!

Peter asked Jesus just such a question. In Matthew 18:21 he asked Jesus, "Lord, how many times shall I forgive my brother or sister who sins against me? Up to seven times?"

Jesus replied in verse 22, "I tell you, not seven times, but seventy-seven times."

Some even translate Jesus' reply as seventy times seven which would equal 490 times!

This activity simply demonstrates the extent Jesus asks us to forgive someone.

Place the large bowl(s) of popcorn in the center of the table. Have everyone begin counting the kernels of popcorn out of the big bowl into their personal, smaller bowls.

For this illustration, we will use "77" as our number (but feel free to be an overachiever and go for 490!)

Once everyone has counted out 77 kernels of popcorn into their bowl, have them take a look at their bowl and ask the following question:

Forgive One Another

"Could you forgive one person 77 times for doing the same thing to you over and over and over?"

Remind everyone that Jesus has done exactly this for us! Jesus' forgiveness knows no end. His grace is boundless.

Now, surprise the kids and go watch a movie together. You already have the popcorn!

77856940R00046

Made in the USA
Columbia, SC
28 September 2017